The Pope from the End of the World

FRANCIS
The Pope from the End of the World

JOSÉ RUÍZ MÁRQUEZ

CLARETIAN PUBLICATIONS
Macao, China

FRANCIS – The Pope from the End of the World

P.O.Box 1608
Macau, SAR, China
Tel: 853-2893-9174
Email: bible@claret.org
www.bibleclaret.org

Nihil Obstat

Rev. Luis Gonzaga Ló
April 11, 2013

Imprimatur
+ José Lai
Bishop José Lai
Diocese of Macau
April 15, 2013

Claretian Publications is a pastoral endeavor of the Claretian Missionaries in Macau. It aims to promote a renewed spirituality rooted in the Word of God and the living tradition of the Church in response to the needs, challenges and pastoral demands of today.

Claretian Publications is part of
CLARET
PUBLISHING GROUP
Bangalore | Barcelona | Buenos Aires | Chennai | Macau | Madrid | Manila | São Paulo

Cover and creative design by: Ian Dacayanan

ISBN 978-99965-876-5-8

"Whatever you did for one
of these least brothers [and sisters] of mine,
you did for me"

Matthew 25:40

DEDICATION

It was 30 years ago that CLARETIAN PUBLICATIONS was born in the Philippines with the pioneering effort of an Argentinean Claretian, FR. ALBERTO ROSSA, who wanted to answer the needs of the time. With more than 1000 titles published and more than 5 millions books sold, Claretian Publications has become one of the main Catholic publishers in Asia.

From the very beginning special attention was given to the Word of God and the publications embarked in an ambitious project: to make the Word of God available in simple yet accurate translation—a Bible accompanied with introductions, notes and commentaries. So the Pastoral Bible was born. The first one, published in 1988, was the Christian Community Bible. With the years the Pastoral Bible was translated and published in 12 more languages.

After spending 27 years in the Philippines, and at 60 years of age, the superiors sent him to open a new front in Macao and Hong Kong. Here Fr. Rossa and several young Claretian Missionaries from India have been working for 7 years. And here too Fr. Rossa started the Claretian Publications Macao to serve the pastoral needs of Chinese Catholics publishing mainly in English, Chinese and Spanish *(for Latin America).*

Today Fr. Alberto Rossa is celebrating 50 years as a religious in the Claretian Congregation. We congratulate him and join him in thanking the Lord for all the blessings of these past years, especially in the field of publications.

This book is then dedicated to two Argentinians: our beloved Pope Francis and to Fr. Rossa as well.

CONTENTS

INTRODUCTION

The election of Cardinal Jorge M. Bergoglio as POPE FRANCIS brought surprise and admiration of people from all over the world. In just a few weeks in office Catholics and people of all faiths have welcomed the new Pope.

He comes *'from the end of the world,'* not only geographically, but also from his clear option for the poor, afflicted and downtrodden.

In an effort to understand his thoughts and spirituality, and to have a sense to where the Church is heading with the new Pope, Claretian Publication is presenting the book: "Francis—*The Pope from the End of the World.*" The book, intended for a wide audience, looks at his family background, to his years of service to the Church in Argentina as Archbishop of Buenos Aires, especially with the poor, the impact of his first weeks as Pope and an interview with his publisher and friend.

Catholics and people from all walks of life have an opportunity to have a glimpse to a true leather, a man of deep faith and courage, a man of power used as service; a man of God who preaches by example and conviction who has surprised all of us with his openness, simplicity and depth.

Jose Lai
Bishop of Macao

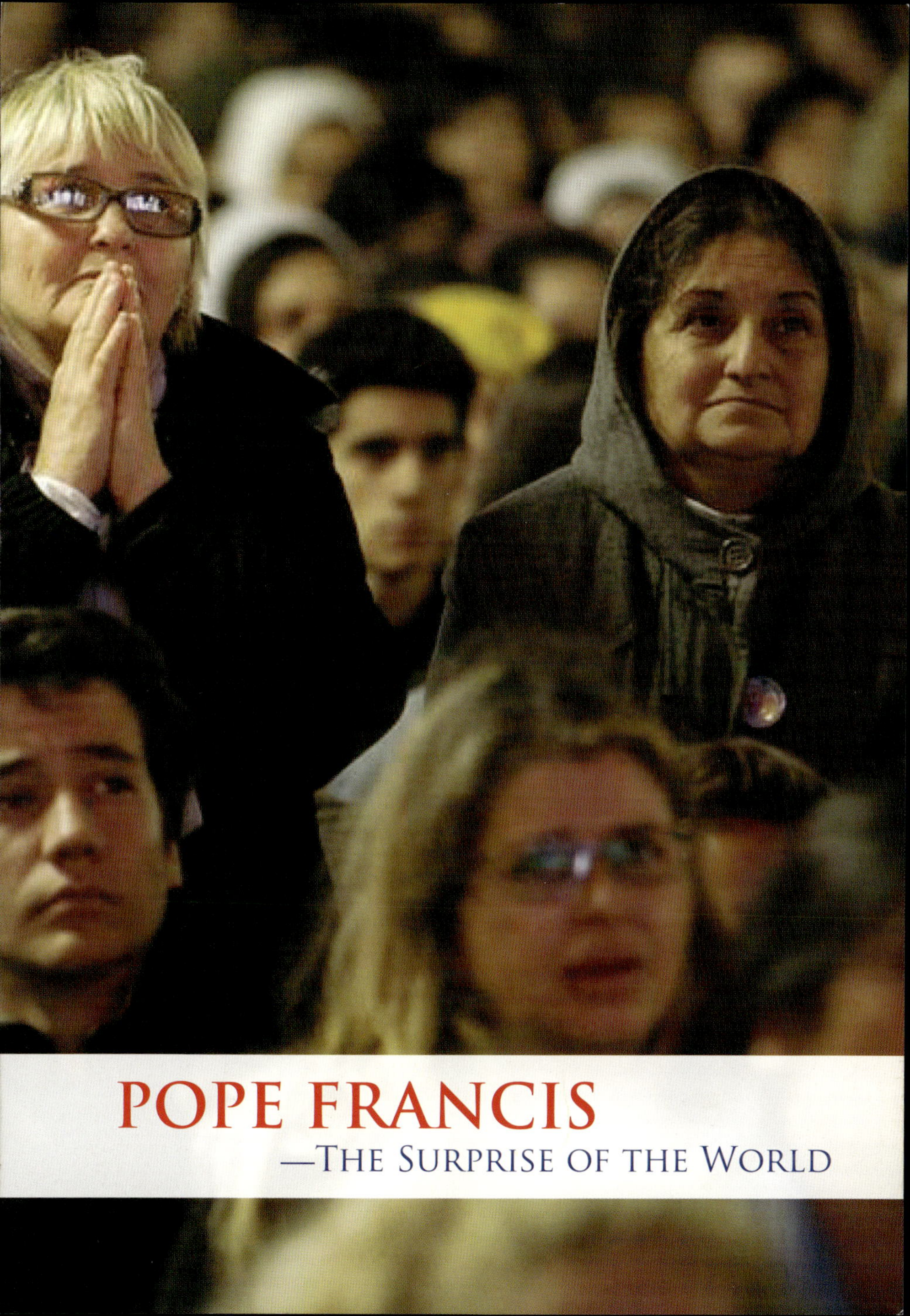

POPE FRANCIS
—The Surprise of the World

A FIRST GLIMPSE

POPE FRANCIS
is a mine of surprises:
the choice of his papal name,
the country he comes from,
the work he has been doing
and above all the way he lives.
The more you walk into his life
from the papal threshold;
you stumble upon pleasant surprises
that plotted in the making of this Pope.
His graceful appearance
that we are acquainted with
through pictures is with a contagious
enthusiasm wrought in his smiles.

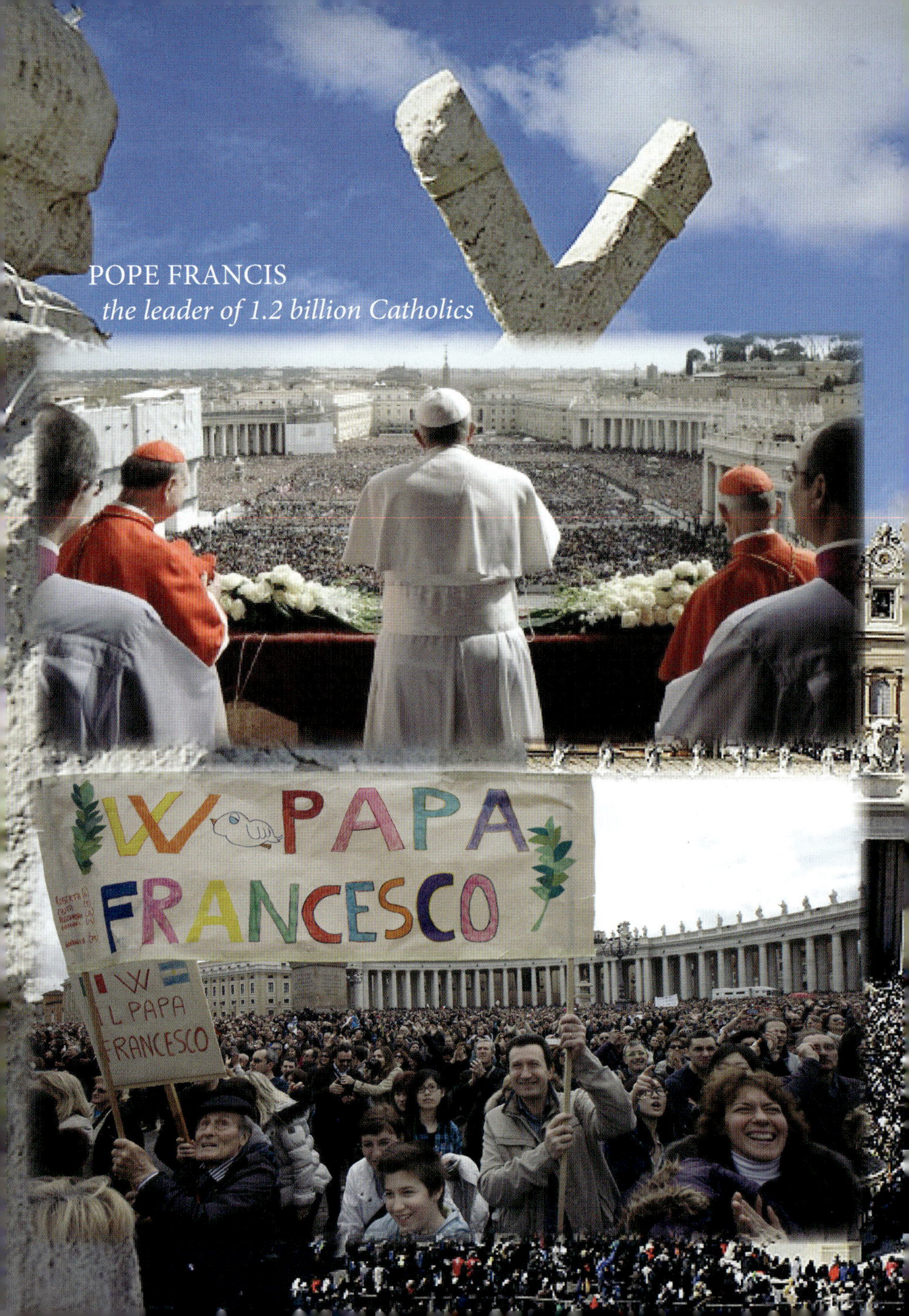

POPE FRANCIS
the leader of 1.2 billion Catholics

THE INAUGURATION

POPE FRANCIS
has officially begun
his papacy as the 266th pontiff,
receiving the RING
symbolizing the office
and a wool STOLE *('PALLIUM')*
symbolizing his role as shepherd
of his 1.2-billion strong flock.

One drawback Pope Francis has in being pope is the printing and circulation of his photos without his permission, and here you have this wonderful picture of his on the cover of this book and the inside pages with his disarming smile already widely known all over the world and wearing the simple cross he has used for years as a bishop. According to his publisher and friend, Claretian Fr. Gustavo Larrazábal:

"He was one of the easiest writers I dealt with as the head of the Claretian Publications in Buenos Aires. When a new book was on the way, Archbishop Bergoglio *used to show up in my office with a bundle of papers in his arms and say, 'Here is all this. Manage it as best as you can.' We, the editors and I in particular, would edit, revise, and send the finished work to him for his approval. He would make his own comments, but the truth is that we were quite free. Our only arguments were over the covers. The cover is very important for me because it is what sells the book. On two occasions, I put his picture on the cover and he was mad. But I said to him, 'Without a good cover the book will not sell. So, you can get mad, but the cover will stay'."*

We, of course, use his picture on the cover of this book not for any commercial purposes, but to introduce Pope Francis to as many people as possible in this part of the world where Christians in general and Catholics in particular are a tiny minority.

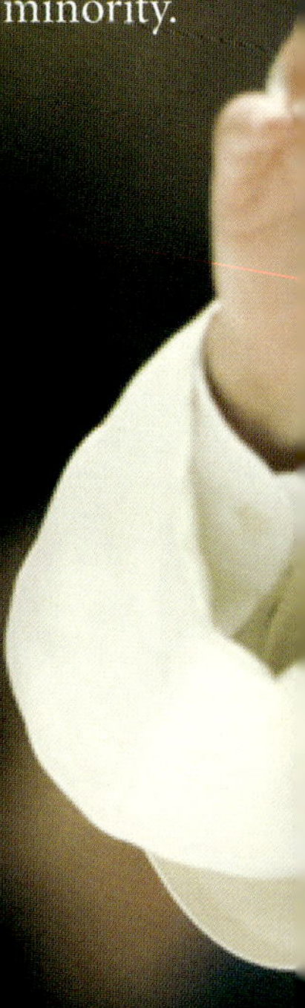

A cheap and opportunistic way of proselytizing, some might say. Of course not, it is something else we want to *"sell"*: his message. Any world leader whether civil or religious, who shows that deep concern as Pope Francis does for the poor and victims of any kind of exploitation, or for a world without war and violence, even against mother nature, is worthy to be made known and be listened to. The commitment to justice, non-violence and respect for nature knows no religious or ideological frontiers. Such a leader is welcome as a fellow-traveler in search of a better world, and therefore belongs not only to Catholics but to all.

POPE FRANCIS

Pope Francis, *where is he coming from and where will he possibly lead the Catholic Church?*

JORGE M. BERGOGLIO, now **POPE FRANCIS** is the 266th and Pope of the Catholic Church, elected on 13 March 2013. As such, he is Bishop of Rome, the head of the worldwide Catholic Church and sovereign of the Vatican City State.

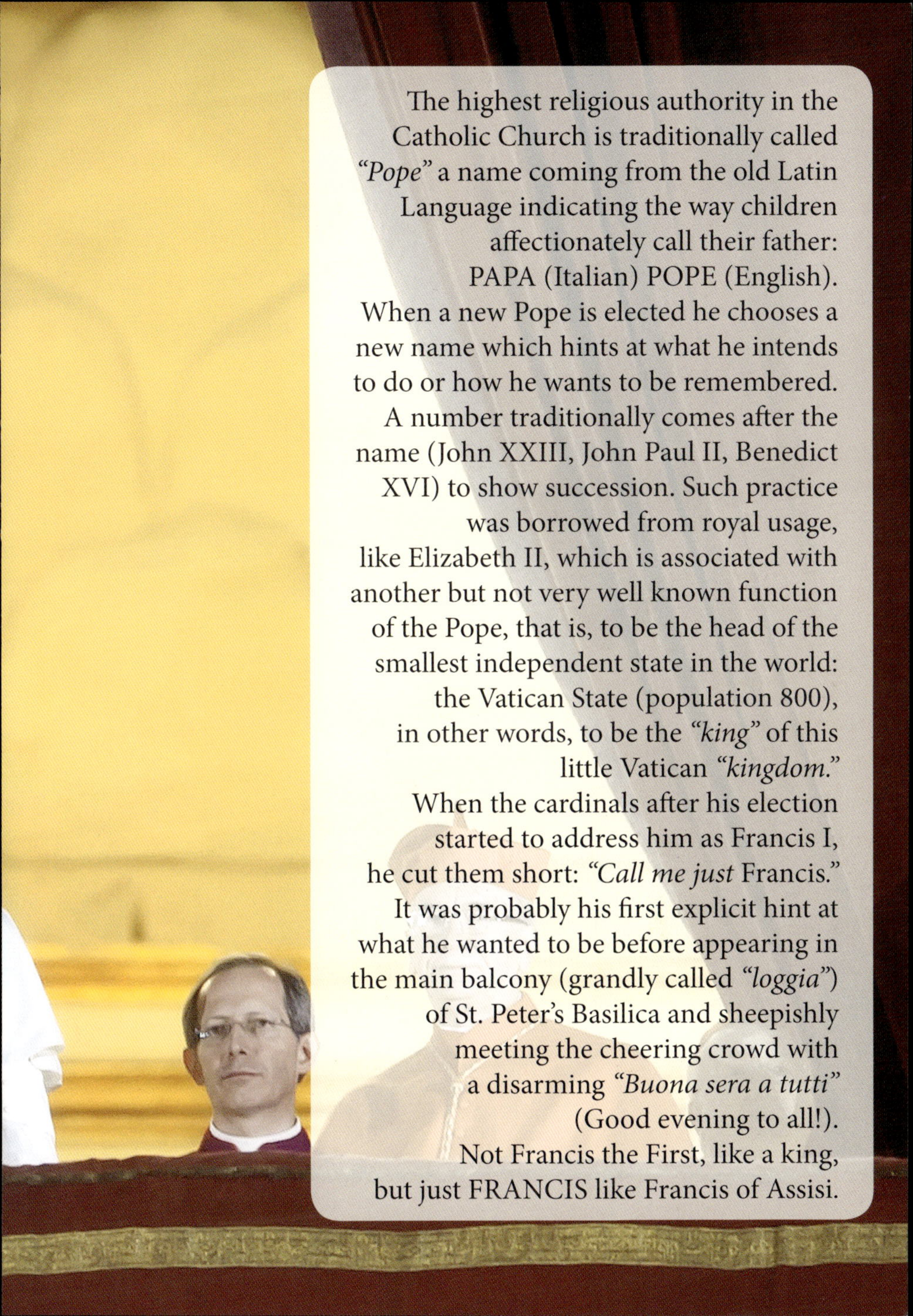

The highest religious authority in the Catholic Church is traditionally called *"Pope"* a name coming from the old Latin Language indicating the way children affectionately call their father: PAPA (Italian) POPE (English). When a new Pope is elected he chooses a new name which hints at what he intends to do or how he wants to be remembered. A number traditionally comes after the name (John XXIII, John Paul II, Benedict XVI) to show succession. Such practice was borrowed from royal usage, like Elizabeth II, which is associated with another but not very well known function of the Pope, that is, to be the head of the smallest independent state in the world: the Vatican State (population 800), in other words, to be the *"king"* of this little Vatican *"kingdom."* When the cardinals after his election started to address him as Francis I, he cut them short: *"Call me just* Francis." It was probably his first explicit hint at what he wanted to be before appearing in the main balcony (grandly called *"loggia"*) of St. Peter's Basilica and sheepishly meeting the cheering crowd with a disarming *"Buona sera a tutti"* (Good evening to all!). Not Francis the First, like a king, but just FRANCIS like Francis of Assisi.

In Rome,
on the way to the conclave

Paying his own bill at the hotel

Francis' *room at the Vatican*

Pope Francis *loves children*

Pope Francis *is a member of football club: SAN LORENZO*

St. Francis of Assisi

FRANCIS is an unusual papal name. It is, in fact, the first time that a Pope chose to be called Francis in honor of St. Francis of Assisi.

The name itself is filled with great symbolism that was instantly welcomed, praised, and commented on around the world by every TV and radio newscaster breaking the news of the election, even before Pope Francis himself explained the meaning of his name to the press.

No papal name in history triggered such an avalanche of enthusiastic comments or raised such hope. Names like "Pius," "John," "Paul," "John Paul," or "Benedict," because of their impact, or the lack of it, would have been met with little surprise or downright indifference by the great majority of Catholics, but not "Francis." In fact, if there is a name that doesn't fit at all the holder of one of the most exalted and prone-to-the-cult-of-personality offices in the world, it is the name of the humble, poor and "*minor*" man of Assisi. The name itself spells already a vision of the Church coming straight from the Gospel which Francis of Assisi embodied in his life and preaching as no other person in history after Jesus. Arguably, it has been said that Francis is the best known Christian after Jesus Christ and his Mother Mary.

Cardinal Bergoglio washes the feet of mothers on Holy Week

…and as Pope he does the same on Holy Thursday.

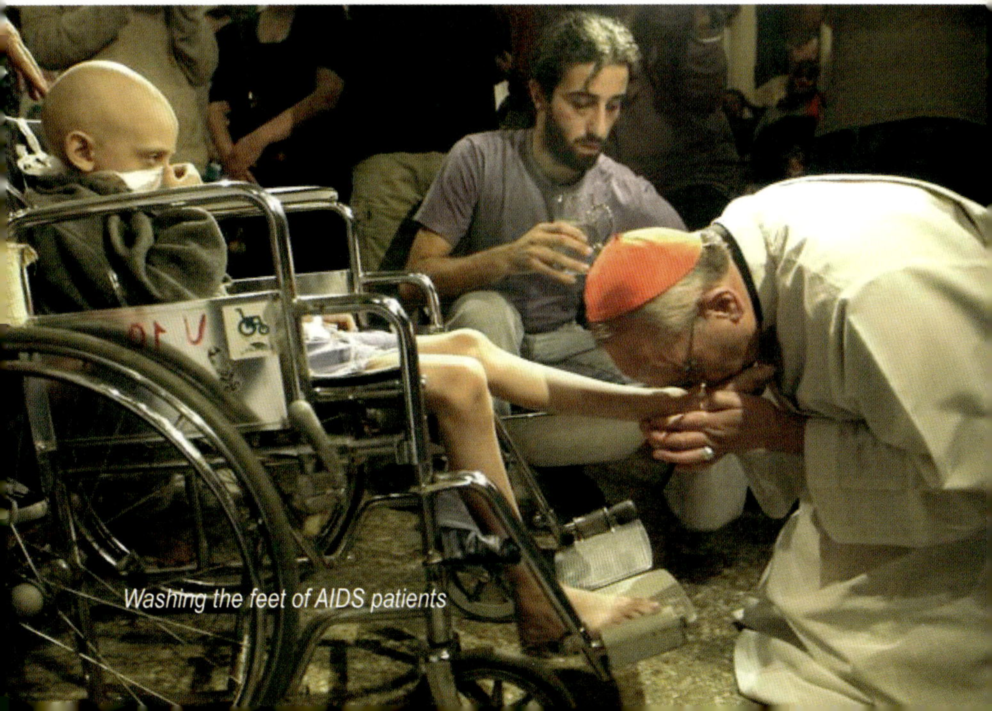

Washing the feet of AIDS patients

Cardinal Bergoglio *took care of protecting people at risk because of their commitment to help others. This woman had infiltrated into a dangerous hooligan band and needed protection.*

No journalist covering the election of Pope Francis failed to mention the *"voice"* which according to tradition *"the Poverello* (the little poor man) *of Assisi"* had heard in the dilapidated small church of St. Damian before he started his life of penance more than 800 years ago: "Francis, *rebuild my church.*" And rebuild he did, literally and with his own hands at first, and, then, living and preaching the values of the gospel, *"sine glossa"* (without interpretation or compromises) as he used to say in poverty and humility. In a 13th century Christian society brutally divided between the rich and the poor, he decisively sided with the poor, the dispossessed, the sick, the lepers, the *"minors"* of his time. In the midst of an on-going religious war between Muslims and Christians, during the Fifth Crusade (1213-1221), he not only took an anti-war stand and preached something revolutionary at that time, that is, the evangelical mandate of non-violence, but took the bold, dangerous, and scandalous step of going personally to talk peace with the Muslim sultan of Egypt, a gesture that almost had him excommunicated by some Church authorities. This and much more is St. Francis, one of the most inspired poets of his time whose famous *"Canticle of All Creatures"* is a challenging *"manifesto,"* inviting us all to protect, love and respect mother nature.

All these images of St. Francis of Assisi must have crossed like a flash in the mind of the newly elected Pope when he was ritually asked by the president of the Conclave for his papal name. He himself explained it, later on, in his first encounter with the journalists: *"Some did not know why the bishop of Rome wanted to be called* Francis. *I will tell you the story. During the election I was seated next to the Cardinal emeritus of São Paulo* Claudio Hummes, *a great friend of mine. When the election began getting a little "dangerous" he started comforting me. And when the votes were up to two-thirds and the usual applause started because a new Pope was about to be elected, he hugged me and said: 'Do not forget the poor' and that word entered here* (pointing to his head): *the poor, the poor. Then, just in relation to the poor I thought of* Francis *of Assisi. Then I thought of wars while the poll was still going on until all the votes were counted... and of* Francis *as a man of peace, who loved the Creation... And of us who have not so good a relationship with Creation, right? And again of* Francis, *the man with the spirit of peace, the poor man ... Oh, how I wish a Church of the poor and for the poor."*

St. Francis of Assisi
defending the poor...

A POPE from the End of the World

..."And it seems that they went almost to the end of the world to find him"

Perhaps one day Pope FRANCIS will tell us if this very first remark about his election pronounced before the multitude filling St. Peter's Square was just a casual or an intentional remark.

It seems too solemn an occasion, his first *"urbi et orbi"* greeting (to the *"city"*, his diocese as a Bishop of Rome, and to the *"world"*, the horizon of his ministry as a Pope) not to measure every word or imply any nuance behind the apparently casual words.

Let us presume that it was an intentional one, whether consciously or unconsciously said.

Let us assume, also, that it was not mere geography he was talking about, and explore this *"end of the world"* he came from in order to take possession of one the most important *'center-stages'* of the world as the new Pope.

Cardinal Bergoglio
at an open square in Buenos Aires.

Could the end of the world be Argentina, one of the biggest countries on earth with a total area of 2,780,400 km2 and potentially one of the richest? Or could the end of the world be the great, cosmopolitan Buenos Aires, the so-called *"Paris of the Americas"*?

Hardly the end of the world, we would say... Or maybe yes, because if you are living in *"Villa 21,"* the infamous, congested, poor, violent slum of Buenos Aires (there are 11 slums like this in the capital city alone) then, Argentina and Buenos Aires are truly the *"end"* of that *"world"* many of us take for granted, that is, mostly prosperous, beautiful, peaceful, secure, in other words, a comfortably normal world.... Beyond that *"end"* begins another world, the *"existential periphery"* as Pope Francis calls it, the home of hundreds of millions of destitute people around the world, because *"Villa 21"* is not only in Buenos Aires but also in Jakarta, Nairobi, Lagos, Mexico City, New Delhi, Manila, Los Angeles and many more.

What if Pope Francis meant precisely this *"end of the world"* when he mentioned in reference to the cardinals who elected him, *"And it seems that they went almost to the end of the world to find him"*?

What about if he came from this end of that world precisely in order to invite the Church, already as Pope, to go to that world where he came from as Archbishop of Buenos Aires?

"Those who know his mind best say Bergoglio *wanted to send a message to the villas: Even if politics and the economy have forgotten about you, the church hasn't. His option for places such as this wasn't notional, a matter of a few lines in a pastoral plan. It took flesh and blood in his penchant for walking the streets, talking to the people, leading them in worship and standing with them when times were tough," says* John Allen *writing for* National Catholic Reporter.

Slum 21 in Buenos Aires. The place often visited by Cardinal Bergoglio

"I'd say that over the 15 years he's been walking down the streets here, at least half of the people have met him at some time and have a picture with him, meaning at least 25,000 people in this villa alone,"... the cornerstone of the new pope's vision is his desire for a "missionary church, one that moves out of the sacristy and into the streets," said bishop Jorge E. Lozano, *a close friend of* Bergoglio.

Mass
at a train station
in Buenos Aires

He often said and wrote:

"The Church has to come out of herself, and to go to the peripheries, not only geographically, but also the existential peripheries where we find the mystery of sin, of pain, of injustice, of ignorance and indifference to religion, and of all miseries."

One of his closest collaborators states, *“one of* Bergoglio’s *major pushes as archbishop was the increase of the Church’s presence in the slums of Buenos Aires. Under his leadership the number of priests assigned to work in the slums doubled. Poverty, child-labor and sexual exploitation have been the main battle he fought together with his priests to the point of publicly calling Buenos Aires in 2003 ‘a sinful city’.”*

“There are poor people in the street and rich people feasting lavishly.”

Jorge Fernández Díaz, a columnist and Secretary of drafting of Buenos Aires’ newspaper La Nación describes Archbishop Bergoglio in this way:

“He does not belong to the oligarchic Church but to the Church on foot. The work he has done in the slums, one of the major problems of the country, is impressive, especially in the infamous “Villa 21”, one of the most populous and violent of Argentina with a gigantic army (10% of the population) of drug-dealers, robbers and traffickers on persons, the present slave-traders.”

"Bergoglio *wanted to bring the 'peace of the souls' to the poorest 'villas' (slums),*" said Fr. Guillermo Torres, the head representative of the Church in "Villa 31," commenting on the election of Pope Francis to a reporter who wrote: *"It is cold in* Guillermo's *chapel. Poverty is all around: the plastic flowers (no money for natural ones), the corrugated iron roof, the cement-cracked floor, 'but for the people of the "Villa"'*—says Guillermo—*'God is as present as in the most important cathedrals... therefore these people feel that* Pope Francis *belongs here more than to "on the other side" because it was here and it was in Villas 21 and 24 where* Jorge Bergoglio *started his work of "Pastoral Villera"* (ministry in the squatter areas which gathers and coordinates all the "villero-priests" [squatter-priests]).'

With Father Pepe, one of the slum priests

According to Fr. Juan Isasmendi, *who lives and works in one of the slums, this is where the future* Pope Francis *filled his lungs with the "oxygen" he needed to think about what the church ought to be. Now that he's* Francis, *perhaps this "Pope of the Villa" (slums) can spread that vision well beyond the borders of Buenos Aires, helping it take flesh all over the world.*

Villa 21-24 is a slum so dangerous that most outsiders don't dare to enter. But residents say Jorge Mario Bergoglio *often showed up unannounced to share laughs and sips of mate, the traditional Argentine herbal tea shared by groups using a common straw.*

"'*The Archbishop*'—adds Fr. Guillermo—'*never accepted security guards to enter in any of the "villas." He used to come by bus... entering on foot where even the police didn't dare to enter, seeping "mate"* (the ubiquitous Argentina's tea) *with the neighbors and evangelizing them with a constant message: "more education, more work and less addiction." He led for us the way to give up our lives for the poor, strengthening and showing us that the Church never must be indifferent to their needs."* No wonder when the *people of the Villa learned of the election of* Francis, *they came running and crying to the chapel to celebrate.*'"

Mass using puppets at the Cathedral in Buenos Aires

In a pre-conclave conversation with his friend the Cardinal of Havana (Cuba) regarding the characteristics the new Pope should have, Jorge Bergoglio commented *"he should be a man who from the contemplation and adoration of Jesus Christ will help the Church to move outside herself to the 'existential peripheries' because when the Church does not move outside herself to preach the Gospel she becomes self-referential, a kind of theological narcissism.*

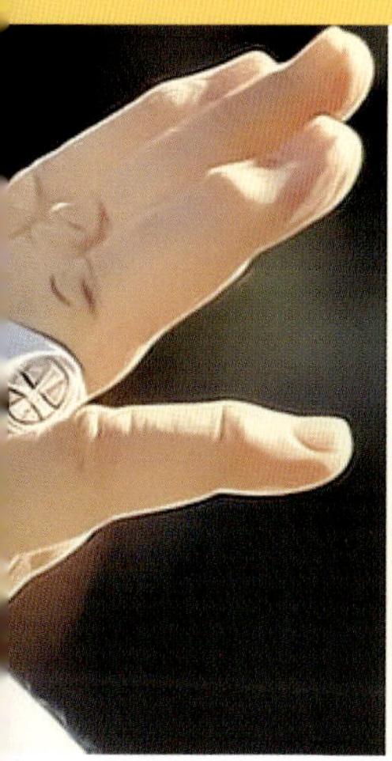

Pope's silver ring, old shoes and old cross ..."You don't change at 76!"

"When the Church does not come out of herself to evangelize, she becomes self-referential and then gets sick. The evils that time and again happen in ecclesial institutions have their root in the 'self-referentiality'."

The 'slum priests' appointed by Cardinal Bergoglio *to live with and attend to the very poor*

Street of one of the slums in the capital

Making an interesting remark on the well-known passage of the book of Revelation (cf. Rev 3:20) he added: *Jesus says that he is at the door and knocks. Obviously, the text refers to his knocking from the outside in order to enter but I think about the times in which Jesus knocks from within so that we will let him come out. The self-referential Church keeps Jesus Christ within herself and does not let him out.... It is the worst evil that can befall the Church: to live within herself, of herself, for herself."*

Fr. Pepe di Paola, one of the most visible *"cura-villero" (slum-priest)* commented to the newspaper El Tribuno:

"Argentina should not fail to take advantage of the election of Bergoglio *as Pope. The people who felt most happy at his elections were those from the 'villas'. I saw it in the Plaza de Mayo."*

The "villeros" (slum dwellers) showed Bergoglio's *pictures of blessing them, baptizing them, taking "mate" with them, as if to say: 'we are proud that this man who used to come and visit us is now the leader of the Church.' The people were really happy and it demonstrates that what we, the priests, saw in him was true, because we may say one thing but if the people from the Villas feel differently, the matter remains between the priests only. But, when you see the simple folks of the Villas feel proud about Pope Francis it means that he was really part of their lives... Not only in the "villas" can be made an option for the poor. I think there is a "look" in* Bergoglio *which coincides with ours: to see the poor not as somebody we have to help but as persons we can learn from. They are open to God as they are not conditioned by material things. I like the Pope's phrase talking about the mission of the Church: 'I don't want a pious NGO'. We don't go to do good and then leave. We must get involved with the poor from the Gospel, from their concrete reality."*

Cardinal Bergoglio *with Father Pepe at slum 21*

What we expect from Pope Francis

A well known author and biblical scholar,
Dolores Aleixandre,
wrote an open letter to Pope Francis,
expressing quite well the sentiments and the hopes
of the millions of Christians, who greeted with
enthusiasm his election, and their dream
of a renewed Church under his leadership:

"Brother Francis, I never thought I would address a Pope like this, but since in your initial greeting you did not call us 'sons and daughters' but 'brothers and sisters,' I feel I have the permission to do so. In the same way it is 'you,' but full of respect, that comes out spontaneously rather than 'Your Holiness' because I cannot imagine calling a true brother 'Your Holiness.'

"In the March 14 issue of the Argentine newspaper 'La Nación' I read that your election has been 'balsamic' which I consider the perfect adjective to describe that which has been happening to us since you greeted us from the balcony of St. Peter's Basilica with a tone both of shyness and trust.

"First balsamic effect: We see you relaxed and fond of joking (what a wonder, a Pope with the sense of humor!), without giving the least impression of being weighed down by the overwhelming and disproportionate responsibility that Popes have been throwing on their shoulders as if they were the only ones in charge of the universal Church, as if other Shepherds did not exist, as if the People of God were a burden to be shouldered and not a community of women and men capable of initiatives and ready to cooperate as we dreamed with Vatican Council II.

"You, instead, have begun to convince us that it is in our company you want to travel along the road you just started. What a way,

so Franciscan for its simplicity and so Ignatian for its lucidity, to point out to a new way of being Church! So we welcome this new task of returning to the freshness of the Gospel and the radicalism of its words.... We are already realizing that as far as the poor are concerned you are not going to give us any respite.

"Your road starts at a time of extreme weakness of the Church. Like the young man who escaped naked from the garden, she has been stripped of all the garments with which she used to protect herself: secrecy, hermetic façade, concealment, negation of what is evident. But it is precisely now, appearing naked and vulnerable before the judging eyes of the world, that, unexpectedly, a marvelous occasion is offered to her: to don, finally and solely, the garment of the glory of his Lord.

"You entrusted us with the task of sustaining you with our prayers, and we are already asking the Lord to give you a few things to start with: patience with the press that tracks your every move.... We also ask that the huge expectations you awaken would not burden you a little too much and that you would feel very free (and very able as well) to select the persons you think can help you in the governance of the Church no matter what might happen to the Curia. You will encounter many stones along the way, criticism, resistance, and you may even stumble. So follow the recommendation of your beautiful homily on the day of St. Joseph, and try to take care of yourself. They went looking for you almost to the end of the world and it has been a wise move. Thank you for accepting! Many of us feel responsible now to pray for you even if we don't belong to your diocese but are happy to know that you also are in charge of caring for the Universal Church. Suddenly it makes sense again to call Pope the Bishop of Rome. May the Lord bless, guard and pour on you the balm of his peace.

Dolores Aleixandre

A Pope from Argentina

Roman Catholics celebrate the election of Argentine Cardinal Jorge Bergoglio *as the new pope at the Metropolitan Cathedral in Buenos Aires.*

ARGENTINA

A Brief Presentation

Argentina is the eighth-largest country in the world in land area and the largest among the Spanish-speaking nations.
It is one-third of the size of China in land area. It has 40 million people with a density of population 10 times smaller than China.

Argentina has long been a melting pot for a wide range of cultures. Being one of the largest Italian and Spanish diasporas Argentina is home to other European ethnics as well. The Asian population in the country numbers around 180,000 of whom most are of Chinese descent. The *de facto* official language of Argentina is Spanish, usually called *castellano* (Castilian) by Argentines.

POPE FRANCIS was the Archbishop of Buenos Aires (1998-2013), the capital of Argentina, with 3 million people, of whom about 90% are Catholics.

BERGOGLIO:
Family of Immigrants

Regina *and* Mario Bergoglio, *wedding day, in 1935, a year before the birth of* Jorge. (Reuters and AP)

The Pope's parents, Mario Bergoglio and Regina María Sívori, both Italian immigrants, met at a mass in Buenos Aires, the capital of Argentina and married later on.

On December 17, 1936 was born Jorge Mario, the eldest of the five children of the family. About his childhood, the newly elected leader of the Catholic Church had declared that *"we just had enough, we had no car or summer vacations, but we did not lack what was necessary"*.

His parents were both good Catholics and hard working; his father was an accountant and his mother housewife, and both spoke in Italian to their children.

Jorge *(left) & his brother* Oscar *who passed away already.*
Archives, (Reuters and AP)

Don Bosco school*:* Jorge Mario Bergoglio*, circled (4th from left, middle row), studied Chemistry before joining the priesthood.*

The POPE
Adolescent Years

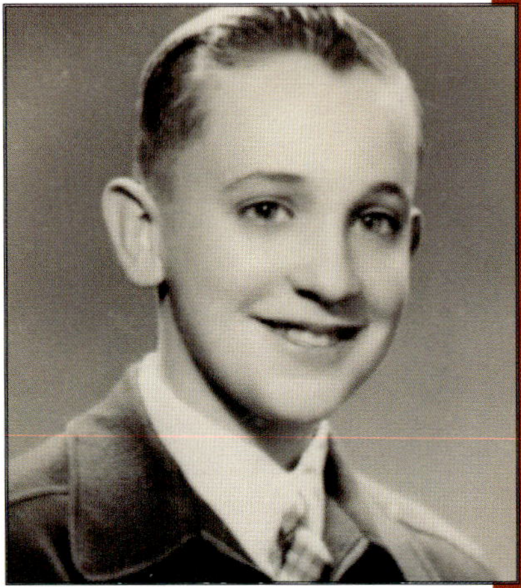

Young Jorge Mario Bergoglio

He attended the school in his neighborhood and for many years kept a correspondence with one of his teachers, Estela Quiroga, who died in 2006 at the age of 96.

He liked sports, played basketball flat-footed as he was. The family with the five children, Jorge, Oscar, Marta, Alberto and María Elena, the only one still alive, often went to a soccer stadium to watch *'San Lorenzo,'* their favorite team playing.

BERGOGLIO *family:*
(L-R) Alberto, Jorge Mario, Oscar, Marta, *and (seated)* María Helena *with* Regina *and* Mario, *their parents.*

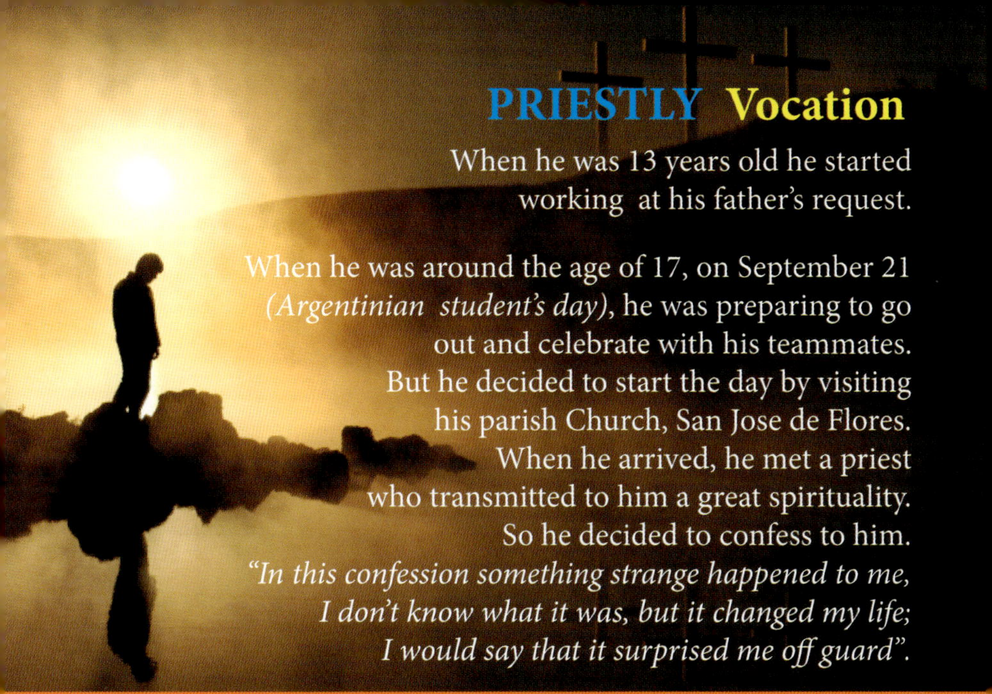

PRIESTLY Vocation

When he was 13 years old he started working at his father's request.

When he was around the age of 17, on September 21 *(Argentinian student's day)*, he was preparing to go out and celebrate with his teammates. But he decided to start the day by visiting his parish Church, San Jose de Flores. When he arrived, he met a priest who transmitted to him a great spirituality. So he decided to confess to him. *"In this confession something strange happened to me, I don't know what it was, but it changed my life; I would say that it surprised me off guard".*

More than half a century later he interpreted it thus:

"It was the surprise, the stupor of a meeting; I realized that somebody was waiting for me. That is the religious experience: the stupor of being with someone who is waiting for you. Since that time for me, God is the one who 'entraps' you. You are looking for him, but He is the one who looks for you first. You want to find him, but He finds us first."

This was the moment he identified his vocation. He decided to keep it quiet until he was completely sure. He graduated from College as a chemistry technician and worked in a laboratory in Buenos Aires.

"First, I told my dad and he received the news very well. But my mom's reaction was different. The truth is that my mom was angry."

(The Jesuit. Conversations with Cardinal Jorge Bergoglio, SJ., Sergio Rubín and Francesca Ambrogetti, Editorial Vergara, pp. 45-47).

At age 21 he decided to enter the Seminary of the Jesuits. At the same time he suffered a severe pneumonia that ended in the surgical removal of a lung, reducing his physical ability forever. Since then, he devoted himself to deepen his studies of Greek literature, Latin and history.

Jorge Mario Bergoglio, *young priest*

Jorge Mario *and his parents,* Regina *and* Mario. (Reuters and AP)

Outsider in the CURIA

In 1969, at age 32, he was ordained priest. The following year he traveled to Spain, to the Jesuit home of Alcalá de Henares.

In 1973 he professed his final vows and by that midyear, with only 36 years of age, he was elected the Provincial head of the Jesuit Order in Argentina, serving until 1979, coinciding with the first three years of the dictatorship of Jorge Rafael Videla.

Fr. Jorge Mario Bergoglio, SJ *(center), then provincial head of the Jesuit Order*

In 1980, he assumed duties as rector of the Faculty of Philosophy and Theology of San Miguel, and as pastor of St. Joseph Parish, in the Diocese of San Miguel, Buenos Aires.

In 1986, he left for Germany, to conclude his doctoral thesis and then he was appointed to the school El Salvador in Buenos Aires.

In 1990, he took over as director and confessor of the Church of the Jesuits in Córdoba, where he worked for two years.

Metropolitan Cathedral of Buenos Aires.

Until 1992, Bergoglio was an outsider within the Curia of his country, but that year he was appointed Auxiliary Bishop of Buenos Aires. The appointment caused surprise, as Bergoglio did not have a *"career"* within the Church hierarchy.

In 1998, when Cardinal Quarracino died, Bergoglio became the first Jesuit in command of the Buenos Aires Archdiocese. As Archbishop of Buenos Aires, Bergoglio created new parishes and restructured the administrative offices of the archdiocese, led pro-life initiatives, and created a Commission on divorces.

LOW Profile

People say he is a good cook

But he did not change his habits: in fact, he continued to travel by bus and subway, continued cultivating a low profile living in the priestly home. He didn't move to the Archbishop's residence. The austerity and low profile living have been the hallmarks of his administration, to the point that in 2001, when he was appointed Cardinal he ordered the faithful not to go to Rome for official acts and allocate the money to the poor.

Entering the Metro station in Buenos Aires

On the Metro, on his way to the pastoral work

Archbishop of Buenos Aires
- his preferential option

Argentine Cardinal Jorge Mario *Bergoglio blesses residents of the Villa 21-24 slum inside the Virgin of Caacupe chapel, in the Barracas neighborhood of Buenos Aires*

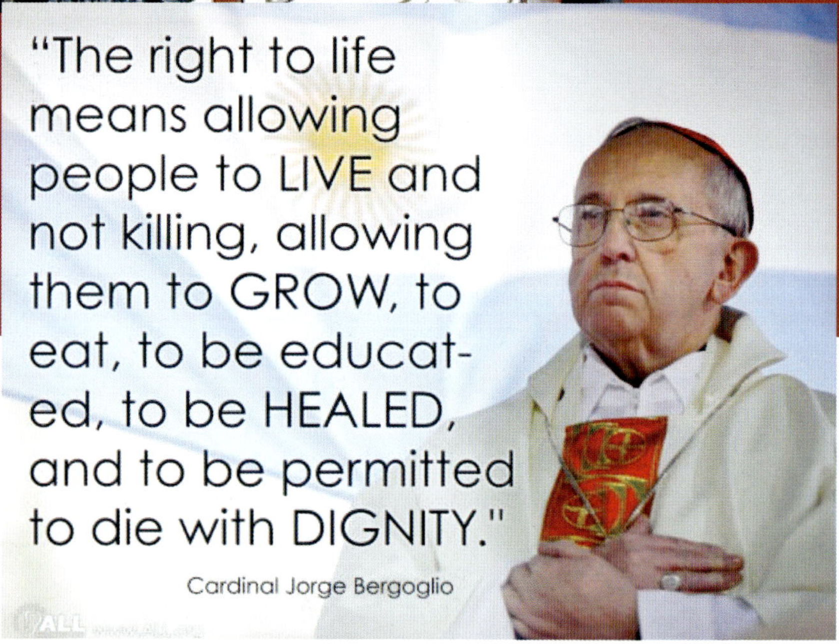

Getting To Know
Pope Francis' Favorites

A book that will soon be available in English:
"Pope Francis: Conversations with Jorge Bergoglio"
by Sergio Rubin and Francesca Ambrogetti, originally published in 2010 under the title ***"El Jesuita"*** ("The Jesuit") reveals some of Pope Francis' favorite things:

☛ Favorite SPORTS:

When he was young, the future pope played basketball, but he loved going to the stadium to watch soccer with his whole family to see their favorite team, San Lorenzo. He lamented that the fan scene today is not what it used to be. At worst, *"people would yell at the referee that he was a bum, a scoundrel, a sellout ... nothing in comparison to the epithets they use today,"* he said.

☛ Favorite CITY:

"I love where I live. I love Buenos Aires."
He has traveled across Latin America and parts of Europe, including Ireland *"to improve my English."*
However, he said, *"I always try to avoid traveling ... because I'm a homebody"* and got homesick easily.

☛ Favorite way TO STAY INFORMED:

Newspapers. He said he turned on the radio only to listen to classical music. He had thought he'd probably start using the Internet like his predecessor, the late-Cardinal Juan Carlos Aramburu of Buenos Aires, did

-- *"when he retired at 75."*

☛ Favorite mode of TRANSPORT as Cardinal Archbishop of Buenos Aires:

The subway, which he would always take to get around *"because it's fast; but if I can, I prefer the bus because that way I can look outside."*

☛ Favorite PASTIME:

As a boy, he liked to collect stamps.
Today, *"I really like reading and listening to music."*

☛ Favorite AUTHORS and BOOKS:

"I adore poetry by (Friedrich) Holderlin," a 19th-century lyric poet; Alessandro Manzoni's *"The Betrothed" ("I Promessi Sposi"),* which he said he has read at least four times; Dante Alighieri's *"The Divine Comedy"*; and anything by Fyodor Dostoevsky and Argentine writer Jorge Luis Borges.

The pope recalled that even though Borges was an agnostic, *"he'd recite the 'Our Father' every evening because he had promised his mother he would, and died with a sense of 'religious comfort.'"*

☛ Favorite MUSIC:
"*Leonore*" Overture No. 3 by Ludwig van Beethoven conducted by the late-Wilhelm Furtwangler, *"who, in my opinion, is the best conductor of some of (Beethoven's) symphonies and works by Wagner."*

☛ Favorite DANCE STYLE:
Tango, which he said he loves *"very much. It's something that comes from within."*
He said he danced the tango when he was young *"even though I preferred the milonga,"* which is an older form of tango with a faster rhythm.

☛ Favorite MOVIE:
"Babette's Feast" because it shows the transformation of a group of people who took denial too far and didn't know what happiness was", he said. *The sumptuous meal helps free them from their fear of love,* he said. He also likes Italian neorealism films, which often confronted the social, economic and moral consequence of World War II, but added that as archbishop he didn't have much time to go to the movies.

☛ Favorite PAINTING:
"*The White Crucifixion*" by Marc Chagall. The scene *"isn't cruel, rather it's full of hope. It shows pain full of serenity. I think it's one of the most beautiful things Chagall ever painted."*

The White Crucifixion

☛ Favorite PERSON:
His grandmother Rosa,
who helped raise him when he was little,
taught him his first words of Italian
and passed on her
deep religious sensibility.

☛ Favorite SAINT he turns to
in time of need:
St. Therese of Lisieux.
He kept a photo of her on his
library shelf with a vase
of white roses in front of it.
"When I have a problem I ask the saint, not to solve it, but to take it in her hands and help me accept it."

St. Therese of Lisieux.

☛ Favorite VIRTUE:
*"The virtue of love,
to make room for others
with a gentle approach.
Meekness entices me enormously!
I always ask God
to grant me a meek heart,"* he said.

☛ Worst VICE to AVOID:
"The sin that repulses me most is pride"
and thinking of oneself as a big shot.
He said when it has happened to him,
*"I have felt great embarrassment and
I ask God for forgiveness because
nobody has the right to behave like this."*

☛ Typical REACTION to unexpected announcements:
He freezes.
When Pope Francis
was elected pope and appeared
at the central balcony,
many noticed he looked
rather stiff.
Turns out that's how he reacted
when he was named auxiliary
bishop in 1992
and how he reacts
"to anything unexpected,
good or bad,
it's like I'm paralyzed," he said.

☛ Things he would RESCUE in event of a FIRE:
His breviary and appointment book,
which also contains all of his contacts,
addresses and telephone numbers.
"It would be a real disaster to lose them."
"I'm very attached to my breviary;
it's the first thing I open in the morning
and the last thing I close when I go to sleep."

He also keeps tucked safe between its pages
his grandmother's letters and her last words
to her grandkids before she died.
She said that in times of sadness,
trouble or loss, to look to the tabernacle,
"where the greatest and noblest martyr is kept,"
and to Mary at the foot of the cross
so that they may *"let fall a drop of salve*
on the deepest and most painful wounds."

A cartoon is worth
more than a thousand words.
Here are some on Pope Francis:

www.kath-Z-30.de
?
?
?

MikeKeefe intoon.com 2-15-13
HE TOOK THE BUS.
PEDOPHILIA
SCANDAL
ABUSE
caglecartoons.com

62

An INSIDE look at Pope Francis

Claretian Father Gustavo Larrazábal, an old friend of Pope Francis, talks about the pope's past in Argentina and what it means for the future of the church.

Fr. Gustavo Larrazabal, an Argentine Claretian missionary, has been the publisher of the books of Cardinal Bergoglio, now Pope Francisco, during all his years as Archbishop of Buenos Aires.

"*Editorial Claretiana*" Buenos Aires, belongs to Claret Publishing Group. The writings of this unknown Pope are now being made available to the rest of the world.

Fr. Gustavo Larrazábal, CMF

How did you meet the new pope?

I met him back in 1997, when he was appointed Archbishop Coadjutor with right of succession in Buenos Aires.
We went to visit the new Archbishop Bergoglio and took a copy of *The Code of Cannon Law* with commentaries as a gift. I remember that it was a simple interview.
He was behind a simple desk in his office. Some time later, in a meeting with other Catholic publishers, the Cardinal commented on that interview humorously, "*The first time that* Gordo *(the chubby one—*Gustavo *is a big man and we all call him '*Gordo*' as a nickname), visited me, he gave me the "Code of Canon Law," thinking, perhaps, that I was ignorant and that I needed to study Canon Law better...*". I remember fondly that first meeting.

That was an interesting story...

The second time I met Bergoglio was in a more difficult situation. That was the time when I began to forge a close relationship with him. He was of great help to me in moments when we had difficulties as a publisher. From Rome, the Holy See, contacted us with a few negative comments about a book we had published. The cardinal called me to help and asked for some clarifications about the book. He was the ecclesiastical authority of the place where I was the publisher. He intervened in an extraordinary, careful way, helping to solve the problem. The cardinal called and asked me: *"Gordo, what is this book about?"* I told him: *"But if you remember, bishop... I sent it as a gift to all the bishops..." (laughs).* The truth is that he helped me a lot. From Rome they were putting a lot of pressure, and Bergoglio, in a very paternal and fraternal way, helped us out of trouble and to realize that the book had some edges that needed to be polished....

From that time on, we started a close relationship, which lasts until today. The day I turned 50 years old, about a year ago, I celebrated Mass with my friends, the editorial staff and family. They had hidden it to me that the cardinal would come to concelebrate at the Mass. I didn't want to preside with the

Fr. Gustavo Larrazábal, 50th birthday celebration

cardinal there. But he stood like one more Claretian brother accompanying me. He told me I had to preside because it was my birthday. And so I did. I really enjoyed that day. My mother and my aunt godmother of baptism were also present. The cardinal was very friendly and affectionate with them also and they were enchanted. He had dinner with us and we had a good time. It was a gesture of closeness with me and a moment of overwhelming joy.

And your relationship with him as a publisher?

We offered to publish his writings.
This strengthened, obviously, the good relationship.
He wanted that we be the editors and publishers of his books while he was the Archbishop in Buenos Aires.
So now, we have all the books that he wrote during his time as the pastor in this Archdiocese; books that are now sought after all over the world.
Editorial Claretiana has the rights to all his writings, until the day he became Pope.
Thus a close relationship of author and publisher as welll as institutional relationship, between the Archbishopric of Buenos Aires and the Editorial Claretiana were established.
We have also published many other books on catechesis and otherwise for which we sought his approval.

You have known him well from a close quarters... how would you describe his personality?

I found in him a father and a friend whenever I had to go to him. He is a person who always heard me, helped me find solutions. He was always optimistic, but not naively optimistic. He is, without doubt, a man of great faith and much prayer. His advice was always qualified, as of a spiritual guide: advising, guiding...; a person always seeking solutions, not wanting to abide in the problem. I think this is very important because, after talking with him, myself and others, came out better. I don't know how to explain it, but after talking with him, you would have another perspective to address the problem, a word that he said... or, simply, that he had heard or advised you.

These days people are saying that he is very affable, very cordial. All that is true! That smile that he has is also very natural, but I would still point out to something deeper than this: the ability to understand each person, no matter who they are. He attended to many people, and whoever has been in touch with him is telling the same thing.

On the other hand, there is the ease to meet him. You do not need to ask for an appointment. When I wanted to see him, I simply called him by phone saying: *"Jorge, I want to talk to you, when can you see me?"* And he would ask: *"Is it urgent, Gordo?"*

If I said 'Yes' he would say something like this: *"Well, now I will make a little room… come now, or come tomorrow morning"*, all without too much protocol. Many times to have access to these personalities you have to go through a secretary, ask for an audience, etc. With him it was not necessary and he always facilitated the process.

Going back to the books. Let's talk about the first two that are being translated in many languages. In his homily at beginning of his pontificate, he used the title of one of these books almost as if it were a programmatic slogan, and then he sent it by twitter: *"Service is the real power."*

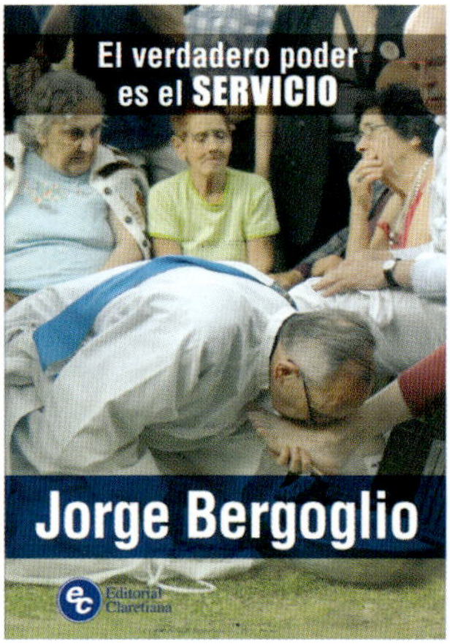

That title was given by our editorial team, obviously taken from one of his writings. He wanted us to prepare a book from his many speeches and homilies. And he edited it. He liked the title and the cover that we prepared with his picture washing the feet of a group of people. The cardinal always gave the final go-ahead to the books, but always gave us freedom to choose the cover. He likes the cover because he said that his face was not seen, only the gesture. We were very happy. It was the same way about the cover of the other book *"Open Mind, Believing Heart."* That he always let us choose the cover, was a sign of his trust. I know that some covers we had on his books did not convince him at all, but he said: *"The decision is yours."*

What about the second book: "Open Mind, Believing Heart"?

The book grew out of a special circumstance. It turned out that the cardinal told me that he had asked the secretary of

the rector of the Catholic University to put some order on his writings because he was already 75 years old. He had presented his resignation and wanted to leave it all in good order. When this person finished the task, it facilitated the work. Regarding those writings, the cardinal said that once the draft was ready we were going to meet and see what we could publish. The material was brought to the editors and we worked, scanning some pages and typing some others that were handwritten. At the end, we saw that we had material for a good book of spirituality and the cardinal approved it. Once this compilation work was completed, we prepared a draft cover that has a beautiful picture of the cardinal. It is with that typical smile, that we all know him now. I sent it to him and told him that he was not going to like it, because his face was very visible. But as he knows me and knows that I am a person difficult to convince; he did not say anything and accepted it gladly. The title of the book is mine. He always likes to repeat that phrase, or something similar. I took it from of one of his lectures, adjusting just a little and asked him: *"What about 'Open mind, believing heart?'* He approved without hesitation at the first sight and that is the history of the title of that book. He told us that it was going to be his last work as Archbishop of Buenos Aires. And now... we have him as Pope. I think that it will be a blessing for the Church, as it has been a blessing in Buenos Aires.

On Easter Sunday, March 31, Pope Francis surprised Fr. Gustavo with a personal call.

FORTHCOMING BOOKS
on Pope Francis by Claretian Publications

A YEAR WITH FRANCIS THE POPE

A selection of 365 quotes from Pope Francis, taken from his homilies since elected Pope and from all his published books. A book that will help the reader, day after day, to walk with Pope Francis, and be in contact with his deep spirituality and call to service.

OPEN MIND, BELIEVING HEART

Reflections, homilies and spiritual retreats preached by Cardinal Jorge M. Bergoglio. The book is a testimony of the priest, spiritual guide and shepherd. The book is a forte for a wide range of audience including priests, religious men and women and laity.
He presents Christian life at the service of God, the world and people. A book that will walk along with the readers in the process of discernment in morals and spirituality.

TRUE POWER IS SERVICE

The writings that this book presents are gathered around some important Christian themes. In the first part deals with catechesis, education, and some texts and reflections on Mary, a key reference in the spirituality of Pope Francis. In a second nucleus there are several of his homilies for Christmas, Holy Thursday, Easter and Corpus Christi. The last part discusses a dialogue with the world of culture. There is an undercurrent in all these texts. It is the key to understanding all of them signified in the title of the book. It deals with the renewal power of service, a revolution based in the social link of service. Power is service.

SIN AND CORRUPTION

Cardinal Bergoglio subtly distinguishes between sin and corruption. He argues that continuous complicity with sin leads to corruption and ultimately to social collapse.

By attending to the dangers of sin and corruption we open ourselves to be transformed by the perfecting and liberating message of the Gospel.

ABOUT SELF BLAME

Cardinal Bergoglio introduces us, in a profound meditation, to the writings of St. Dorotheous of Gaza, and orients us down a path towards humility and love, which are necessary components to form real Christian communities.
He addresses the vice of focusing on others' sins.
To overcome this bad habit, he proposes the practice of self-accusation, in which individuals and communities reflect on their own shortcomings and sins.

TO EDUCATE: CHOOSING LIFE

TO EDUCATE: EXPERIENCE AND PASSION

In these two books, the new Pope speaks to and challenges educators: *How far can we walk without a clear path? Where can we go with no goal to guide our steps? What is the way out of these difficult times the world is facing?* He urges those in academia to form tomorrow's leaders who will guide us towards Christ and his destiny for humanity. And specifically in the fourth volume, he challenges educators to deepen their commitment to teach with passion and zeal as Jesus the master teacher did. This volume will include key readings for individual as well as group study.

A PRAYER for POPE FRANCIS
Jorge Mario Bergoglio, SJ

O God,
shepherd and ruler of all the faithful,
look favorably on your servant Francis,
whom you have set at the head of your Church
as her shepherd.

Grant, we pray,
that by word and example
he may be of service
to those over whom he presides
so that, together with the flock
entrusted to his care,
he may come to everlasting life.
Amen.